Hard Pews, Boring Sermons and No Loos!

Excuses and reasons why people don't go to church

John Cox

kevin
mayhew

First published in Great Britain in 2016 by Kevin Mayhew Ltd
Buxhall, Stowmarket, Suffolk IP14 3BW
Tel: +44 (0) 1449 737978 Fax: +44 (0) 1449 737834
E-mail: info@kevinmayhew.com

www.kevinmayhew.com

9 8 7 6 5 4 3 2 1 0

ISBN 978 1 84867 824 8
Catalogue No. 1501510

Cover design by Rob Mortonson
© Image used under licence from Shutterstock Inc.
Edited by Virginia Rounding
Typeset by Angela Selfe

Printed and bound in Great Britain

Contents

PART 2

PART 3

About the author

Having spent rather a long time at various universities including Cambridge, Oxford and the University College of Rhodesia and Nyasaland, John was ordained to a curacy in the diocese of Liverpool in 1968. He spent a second curacy in an inner-city ex-slum parish in Birmingham and became rector in the same parish. After a five-year period at Church House, Westminster where he was Senior Selection Secretary, helping to select ordinands, he was made Canon Treasurer at Southwark Cathedral and Diocesan Director of Ordinands and Post-ordination training.

Following four years as Vicar of Roehampton he moved to become Archdeacon of Sudbury in the Diocese of St Edmundsbury and Ipswich in 1995. When he retired in 2006 he was asked to be the part-time Diocesan Director of Education, a job he did for nearly four and a half years before retiring for a second time. It has been during these retirement years that John has been writing for Kevin Mayhew, in between being chair of governors at a primary academy, playing golf and enjoying river cruises.

For details of all John Cox's books, please visit our website: www.kevinmayhew.com

Introduction

Clues from the concert hall

Church decline, church growth. Now that gay sex and women bishops aren't quite so much in the headlines, decline and growth are the debating points. Why the decline? How can we grow? It's not, of course, a new topic and it is unlikely that anything that is dazzlingly new will emerge from the debate – certainly no knock-down, instant answers.

The Church isn't the only institution looking to attract newcomers. In July 2015 a story appeared in the press concerning the Hallé Orchestra's attempt to draw in people who didn't usually go to classical music concerts. They put on what they called a 'Priceless Classics' concert. Although tickets were required, they were free. The concert-goers were invited to pay *after* the performance and to give what they thought it was worth. The ten pieces were all carefully timed so that people could come and go as they wished, they could take drinks into the concert hall (something usually banned) and they could get up, walk around, go to the loo. It was concert-going for people 'on their own terms', as John Summers. the orchestra's chief executive, explained. 'We want to do an event that will bring in a new audience. People who thought classical music was not for them or had never been to a concert hall and were kind of scared of the whole rigmarole . . . The whole point is the people don't feel constrained by the normal concert etiquette. If they want to clap, they clap.' In all this it was apparently the male members of the orchestra who had to face the biggest issue: deciding what to wear, as 'tails' were forbidden!

What I found fascinating about this was not merely the fact that it was being tried but the nature of the underlying barriers to attendance that the event was seeking to overcome: cost, fear, formal required behaviour patterns, performers dressed up in strange garb, time constraints. They were doing it with an 'evangelical' concern: to draw in people to something the orchestra believed was good and beneficial and enjoyable but which people just hadn't tried before. It was still a classical concert but with accessible-sized pieces across a range of styles and composers. It was a concert for the 'pick and mix', 'what's it worth?', 'I don't want to be dictated to' culture. It was aimed to be a 'comfortable' experience. Would it challenge? Probably, for some at least, but not too much.

I suggest that here are some clues and parallels for the Church. Not the whole answer by any means and I don't know how many completely 'new'-comers actually went to the concert, but what the Hallé did is worth reflecting on.

At one level the things that put people off going to church are not so different from those the Hallé was trying to overcome. Just the thought of going into a church can be off-putting – will it be dark? will I know what to do? where do I sit? can I talk? will there be a loo? People don't know what will be expected of them but they guess that something a bit strange will be going on. Will they understand it? Will they be expected to do something that will embarrass them? Then there will be those people dressed up in funny clothes and it will probably go on and on and on. 'It's not my sort of thing.'

It's no good regular churchgoers simply dismissing this as excuses or people being silly. These are real issues for some people even if they are, to some extent, at a fairly superficial level. There are plenty of deeper reasons that people have for never darkening the church door – matters of faith and behaviour, issues about hypocrisy and personal worth. Bad past experiences of church can last a lifetime and be off-putting. The reasons for not going to church are various and complex, relating to how things actually are and how they are perceived. It's not just non-believers that don't go to church – there are plenty of people willing to call themselves Christians who don't go either.

This book attempts to explore some of these issues – both at the individual personal level and more widely through questions of culture and social attitudes. The very act of identifying some of the reasons for people being put off the Church may give clues as to how they could be overcome. But there will be some more deeply rooted issues, not least questions that require theological consideration and the part the legacy of the past plays in the present.

How far should the Church go to make it possible for people to go to church 'on their own terms'? Just as the Hallé Orchestra did not drop its classical repertoire and simply offer a pop concert, so it will be suggested that the Church must not forsake its basic message and simply offer some form of generic, populist spirituality.

Figuring it out – some statistics

But first, just a few statistics to give a picture of how things are. All statistics should have some 'health warnings' attached to them, not least because churches base their statistics on different criteria and, as the Humanist Association is anxious to point out, the questions asked in a survey can 'skew' the outcomes. For example, a national census question asks 'What is your religion?' and some people feel that this loads the question with an assumption that a person does, in fact, have a religious affiliation. The 2011 census indicated that 58% of the participants said they were Christian – a decline from 72% in 2001. A YouGov survey of 2011, however, showed that Christian affiliation was only 53%, with 39% having no religion. A British Attitudes survey in 2014 put those with no religion as high as 50.6%.

The percentages may vary but there is no doubting the general trend, especially when seen over a fairly long period of time. UK Church membership (itself a problematic term), as a percentage of the population, has **declined** from 33% in 1900 to 12.3% in 2005 and further down to 11.2% in 2010.[1]

While there is a general fall in membership, it is not evenly spread across the denominations (2005-2010): Church of England: -5%; Roman Catholic: -12%; Methodist: -19%; Baptist: -5%; Presbyterian: -19%. Overall church membership declined by 6%. While the decline

---

1. UK Christianity 2005-2010 overview, in *UK Church Statistics*, ed. Peter Brierley, ADBC Publishers, 2011.

has been greatest in Scotland and Wales, in England the position is more or less static – not least because in some churches membership is actually **growing**: New churches (evangelical and charismatic) +12% and Pentecostal +27%. Among the 600 newly opened Pentecostal churches in the five-year period the majority were black churches, while the major denominations were actually closing churches (Methodist: 310; Church of England: 200; Roman Catholic: 140; United Reformed: 90). The overall figure showed that 1350 churches closed and 1330 opened (2005-2010).

Church attendance has also declined overall. The Religious Trends survey 7 from Christian Research indicated that, while in 1980 11.1% of the population attended religious services, by 2005 this had declined to 6.3%.

In 2014 58.4% said they never attend religious services (British Social Attitudes 2014).[2] Of the 16% of those who say they are Church of England, 51% say they never attend services and only 10% attended in the previous week.

The **Church of England**'s report *Statistics for Mission 2013* indicated that 2% of the adult population were on the electoral roll of CofE churches, a 9% decline since 2007. A comparison of figures for Easter communicants in the Church of England between 1930 and 2013 showed a drop from 8% of the adult population to just 2%, and for Christmas communicants from 6.2% to 2% over the same period. There has been a steady decline in the number of baptisms in the Church of England over the last century, with only 20,000 in 2013. But not all the statistics are gloomy. While the report indicated that 24% of CofE churches showed signs of decline, 19% showed signs of growth.

As a proportion of the population, rural church membership is still higher than in urban areas. But it is in rural churches where decline is most often evident while growth is seen in urban areas, especially among the middle-class suburbs and in the London area. Anglican cathedrals

---

2. See www.bsa.natcen.ac.uk.

have bucked the overall trend with attendance figures showing a 30% rise in the period 2001-2011. This deserves some careful analysis but possible explanations may well be found in the fact that the worship offered, although often quite traditional, is of a high standard; in addition, worshippers can enjoy a level of anonymity if they want it and cathedrals are very good at 'big occasions'.

Overall cathedral attendance at Christmas rose by 15,600, but only about 25% of those who attended were communicants. Easter attendance figures were more or less static over the period. This reflects the general nature of Christmas services – carol services, crib and Christingle services often attract large numbers, many of whom are not regular worshippers. Overall it is estimated that about 10% of the population attend a service in one church or another over the Christmas period.

In other major denominations statistics are not kept in quite the same way but, as we have seen, the picture is similarly one of decline in membership and attendance.

Currently about 9% of the population describe themselves as **Catholic**. Membership of the Roman Catholic Church in England and Wales reached a peak in 1993 at 4.53 million but by 2010 had dropped by 0.5 million. Between 2011 and 2012 the number fell by about 2.2%, with a similar drop in attendance at Mass. It is estimated that only about one fifth of Catholics actually attend Mass. These figures would have been worse but for the level of migration from Eastern Europe. Two disturbing statistics are those for priests and ordinations: between the years 1992 and 2011 the number of priests dropped from 6995 to 5264 (about 25%) and ordinations in the same period from 65 to 16 (by about 77%).

The **Methodist** Church is the UK's fourth largest Christian denomination. Membership in 2014 was 209,000 while in 1980 it was 600,000. The majority of its current members are of retirement age. The demography of church membership is a matter of concern for many churches.

In 2010 the **Pentecostal churches** had 434,905 members, up 27% since 2005 and the **New churches** had 211,025, up 12% since 2005.

In these churches membership is based on attendance, as compared to the Church of England where membership is based on the electoral roll, and attendance includes a higher proportion of occasional worshippers.

If nothing else, these statistics indicate that the picture is more complex than a simple headline announcement of decline. There are cultural and ethnic elements, there is a clear difference between declared allegiance and actual participation in religious services, and there are pockets of growth. These statistics do not say anything about the contact of the churches with their local and wider communities through voluntary work, the influence they have in forming attitudes, the relationship between formal and 'folk' religion. What they do is provide a background to the more anecdotal and narrative content of what follows.

Inevitably, much of what is discussed in the following chapters draws on the experience of the more traditional-style churches where decline has been most noticeable. The New and Pentecostal churches have largely been growing so are not facing the same kind of problems. Their experience may give some clues about what is 'successful' but again the picture is complex, and simplistic answers will not be helpful, since social factors of ethnicity, cultural patterns, history and aesthetics will play a part, as well as theology and questions of organisation, leadership and authority.

PART ONE

ONE

'Kind of scared of the whole rigmarole'

John Summers, the Hallé Orchestra's chief executive

It's not only those who have never been to a classical concert who can be 'kind of scared of the whole rigmarole'. Going to a church service for the first time, especially on your own when you've never been before, can be scary. There are plenty of people who have intended to go to church and got all the way to the door, only to hesitate and turn away again. Their fear has overcome whatever motive it was that first led them to think of going to church. What is it that can make them fearful?

There is, of course, the fear of the unknown. Before you even get as far as the door there may well be 'obstacles' to overcome. Rural churches often have long paths through the churchyard, sometimes more than one, and it is not always obvious which one leads to the main door. The door may well be shut and its large heavy handle clanks. Your entering will be so obvious when you hoped you might be able to slip in unnoticed. Some churches will have more than one entrance and people may appear to be using different ones. Which one should you go through? You don't want to end up in the wrong place.

Having got this far, there is still actually getting into the church. Entering any strange building can raise anxiety. You are not sure exactly where to go. Will there be signs to help you? Are there alarms you might inadvertently set off? It might be dark, so will you be able to see properly? Will it be obvious where you can sit or are there restrictions on that? It doesn't help that everyone else seems so certain about things, so self-assured. It would seem sensible just to ask someone but when you are feeling anxious that is not always as easy as it sounds.

Church buildings vary enormously, from small medieval ones to great gothic cathedrals, from Victorian piles to glass and concrete modern. Some will indeed be dark, others light as a supermarket. Some you stumble straight into, pushing at a heavy old door and down a step or two; others will have reception areas, with offices and doors everywhere and with no clear indication which one leads into the main part of the building. To the regular churchgoer all these things are taken in one's stride with hardly a thought. It's not like that for the stranger. And it's these first impressions and anxieties that are important. The sign on the notice-board outside might assure you that you are welcome – by God, no less – but on its own that will not overcome the anxiety of actually entering. The simple physical act of entering a church takes courage.

How easy is it for a stranger who has never been before to find the right way into your church?

Are there any actual physical reasons making it difficult to enter? Is access easy for all?

Having got inside the building, there's the anxiety of what to do next. Where to sit? Can you sit anywhere? You certainly don't want to be at the front, but there may be ropes across some of the pews at the back. Perhaps they are being reserved for someone? Or the seats may all be in a circle. Do you need some kind of service book? There are a number of different books on a table and pieces of paper. Do you need all of them? Of course most churches don't leave people just to muddle through the best they can – although it is not unknown. There is usually someone to lend a helping hand, offer you the books you need, if in fact you do need any. Being told 'you can sit where you like' may appear friendly but can actually raise anxieties. You are not sure how literally you can take that and you don't want to sit down only to be told that it is the minister's chair, or that's where the music director normally sits.

All this feels a lot easier if you are part of a crowd of people, all of whom may be feeling a bit like you – a funeral or wedding party, for example. But it's the lone visitor who is likely to be most anxious.

Having sat down, the anxieties don't stop. What if people talk to you? What if they don't? How will you know when to stand and when to sit? Will they tell us or should you just follow the person in front? Even that has its dangers. There's a story (said to be true) of a visitor to a Danish church. He didn't know the language but just wanted to be there. He decided to follow whatever the man in front of him did. All went well until the minister asked a question and the man in front stood up. The visitor followed suit and was amazed at the reaction from all around him. It was only afterwards that he realised that he had been at a baptism and the minister had asked who the father of the child was. It was the man sitting in front of him whose actions he had been following.

At some point someone might come near to where you are sitting and hand you a bag or a plate. Some people have been putting money in it, others have put in an envelope. You don't have an envelope, so would a few coins be OK or should you put in more? What's normal in these circumstances?

For someone who has never been to a Communion service before, there are added things to worry about. For a start, there's the sharing of the peace. In some churches this is a signal for everyone to move around greeting and hugging each other. Are you supposed to join in and what is it that you say? Do you really have to kiss everyone or would a handshake be OK? Then the minister invites people to come up to the front to receive communion or a blessing (not quite sure what that means). Do you go up and get it wrong or stay where you are, even though someone keeps urging you to go up? Or else it gets passed round – a small piece of bread and then a glass with some wine in it. Should you take some or not? Do you just pass it on? What are the words they are saying? It's all a bit fraught and anxious-making. It makes you think it must be like being invited to dinner at Buckingham Palace and not having a clue which knife and fork to use. There is a real fear of embarrassment – not only for yourself, but also the fear of not wanting to embarrass others. They said you were welcome, but what happens reinforces the fact that you are an outsider.

Then what about getting out of church? The others are all milling around getting refreshments, talking with one another. You're not sure you do want to talk to anyone and you're not sure you want to be ignored either. Perhaps it would be best just to slip out. But the minister catches you. She wants to be friendly but will insist on asking all sorts of questions.

Not everyone goes through all this, of course, and the more self-confident someone is, the easier it is likely to be. But many who try church for the first time, on their own, are not feeling very confident. They may be troubled, grieving, lonely, guilty, a stranger in that place and just gone in because there was nowhere else open.

It sounds simple to state that a church should be welcoming. And of course many are. But it's not necessarily easy to get it right. Welcomers need to be sensitive not only to what people say but to how they appear, the signs of anxiety they may be giving. Some will like a hearty, chatty welcome but not everyone will. Some would like to be sat next to someone who can show them through the service, others just want to be alone. Being swept along by a boisterous welcome, being invited to be involved in things before they have hardly crossed the threshold may be just what some people would like. They would feel ignored with anything less. But for others it would be overwhelming and they will want to run a mile.

How are welcomers chosen?

How sensitive are they to people's different needs?

Is the 'ministry' of welcome ever discussed in your church?

TWO

'Once was enough for me'

Retail businesses know that getting a customer into the shop once is good but it's only a start. What they want are returning customers – customers who had a good first experience and will go back to spend more, and more and more. Loyalty can't be counted on. It has to be won and continually worked at. For too many people the experience of a church service is not good. For whatever reason, they were willing to 'give it a go' but don't want to make a habit of it. They'll not be returning.

Individual reasons will vary greatly but there are some general pointers that are worth considering and some of them relate to the fears we looked at in the previous chapter.

For some people it's a matter of the building itself, especially if it's an old one. What some find as quiet, peaceful and with a real sense of the spiritual, others see as damp, dark and frankly spooky.

I don't know anyone who finds **pews** comfortable. Some of them seem to have been designed with the express purpose of keeping congregations awake, literally on the edge of their seats. The seats themselves are often too narrow. The backs, far from providing a restful support, catch you in the small of the back and throw you forward. Attempts to provide a bit of comfort by means of seat cushions have limited success. Pews are frankly a bit of a nightmare. English Heritage, the Victorian Society, and heritage-loving villagers all produce their reasons for keeping pews where they are. Others just long to be able to get rid of them – to provide more space allowing flexibility for worship and other events, and to give congregations more comfort.

Having come to terms with the uncomfortable seating there is the matter of warmth or, more usually, **cold**. Again, the modern church has less of a problem here but older churches struggle. Old hot water systems with boilers, cast iron pipes and radiators have often come to the end of their life and were not always very effective in the first place. Attempts are made to replace them with radiant heaters from on high, pew panel heaters or under-pew heating. All of these have their drawbacks, and in too many rural churches no satisfactory solution has been found. We are just not used to being cold in public buildings. Central heating in most homes has raised our expectations and putting on extra layers of clothes is not the answer it once was. Being cold and uncomfortable are not experiences that encourage people to return to church.

Then there is the vexed question of **loos**. There are certainly many elderly people who will just not risk going to a church where they fear there will not be a loo, or know from embarrassing experience that there is not one. Modern churches have no problems here but older buildings, especially medieval ones, present a considerable challenge. Under Disability Discrimination legislation, public places are expected not only to make provision for the physically disabled and those with sight and hearing difficulties but also to take into account questions of 'continence'. However, the legislation only requires what is reasonable and that includes finances. A church is not required to bankrupt itself in order to provide toilets, but this should not be allowed to be an easy excuse for not making the effort.

The siting of a loo in a church is not always obvious. It doesn't want to be at the front and needs to have 'sound proofing'. What can look like a common sense solution can fall foul of either the church or the heritage authorities. And this adds further fuel to people's impression that churches are out of touch and obsessed with rules and regulations.

On the one hand, churches appear to be given every encouragement to make themselves accessible and user-friendly for the community while, on the other hand, every obstacle appears to be put in their way to prevent them from actually bringing themselves into the twenty-first century. Where toilets are provided, they should be clean. It sounds so obvious but not every church even manages this. An old Elsan outside in the churchyard could be worse than a dash behind a bush!

Worship is not entertainment, but what cinema would ever expect to be able to attract customers if it had hard seats, no loos and the temperature never rose above 10 degrees?

How pleasant is your church building to worship in? Is it designed to make people feel comfortable and at ease? If not, what might you do about it?

What then of the actual experience of worship? People aren't stupid but neither are they born with an inbuilt knowledge of what goes on in a church service. What is very familiar to the regular worshipper will be very strange to the first-timer.

If they are attending a service in a traditional church where there is a set **liturgy** – e.g. Anglican or Roman Catholic – there will be the matter of the service book itself. Some churches provide a booklet that simply takes the worshipper through the service. What is on the page is what is said and done. But there are plenty of churches where the book provided requires navigating round in order to find what is actually happening on this particular occasion. Those who lead worship are not always alert to the presence of a newcomer and fail to give guidance about where to find what. Any additions to the written service may add variety for the regular worshipper but only add to confusion for the newcomer. It may be annoying to the regulars when the minister keeps saying which page they are on but it's important in helping the newcomer. Matters are not made easier where there are additional books or sheets – for hymns, readings or whatever.

In a church where the service is much less formal and there is no set order, the anxiety may not be where to find what is happening but what on earth is going to happen next. The more 'interactive' the worship is, the greater the anxiety may be. It's the problem of 'the peace' writ large. Someone who is used to formal worship elsewhere can find the apparent shapelessness of this kind of service disconcerting. They experience something of the sense of strangeness a newcomer feels wherever they go.

The **language** of religion – of services, hymns, and readings – is unusual. Necessarily so, since it is trying to evoke and capture aspirations and experiences, thoughts and feelings which are not mundane, everyday. It has been suggested that the ability of human beings to create language that deals with the non-tangible, non-factual, the spiritual and the mythical is what helped them to advance in creating complex and large social units.[3] The language of religion binds people together. But that is only true if everyone accepts and trusts what is being said, if it is a common language. Much of what is said or sung in church is no longer part of the general language.

We don't speak in seventeenth-century English and yet in some churches where the Book of Common Prayer (BCP) and the King James Version of the Bible are still lovingly used, that is what is heard. 'Thees and Thous' may add resonances of reverence and respect for some but to the majority they are just plain weird. A reading from St Paul can be difficult at the best of times; in an older version it can sound incomprehensible:

Wherefore, as by one man sin entered into the world, and death by sin; and so death passed upon all men, for that all have sinned: for until the law sin was in the world: but sin is not imputed when there is no law. Nevertheless death reigned from Adam to Moses, even over them that had not sinned after the similitude of Adam's transgression, who is the figure of him that was to come. (Romans 5:12-14; Authorised Version). Or take

---

3. See Yuval Noah Harari, *Sapiens: A Brief History of Humankind,* Vintage Books, 2015.

a well-known collect from the BCP: *Prevent us O Lord in all our doings with thy most gracious favour . . .* It only makes sense if you know that in seventeenth-century English 'prevent' meant 'go before' or 'go ahead'. So God is not being asked to stop us doing things but to get ahead of us, prepare the way, be there even before we start.

It isn't only a matter of old styles of speaking. Part of the problem as well as the strength of religious language is that much of it is symbolic or only makes sense if you have the necessary background knowledge to pick up the associations that give the language its fuller meaning. Although Christianity is one of the religions taught in school, many of the younger generation are growing up without a knowledge of the Christian story, its faith statements, its hymns. Even 40 years ago, in a local radio 'vox pop', young people in a Birmingham shopping precinct had no idea who the person was depicted on a crucifix. The girls recognised it as a piece of jewellery but knew nothing of its significance. It was just 'a silver cross with a little bloke on it'.

No wonder then that a common Christian phrase like 'Washed in the blood of the Lamb' is utterly meaningless and actually sounds objectionable or pagan. Some of the most precious and deeply felt spiritual phrases are opaque to the general public. At the heart of the most significant act of worship, the Holy Communion, there is 'the Body of Christ' and 'the Blood of Christ' to be eaten and drunk. Even a regular churchgoer I once knew found this very difficult to take. For him it was a kind of cannibalism. What were once common symbols have become esoteric. There are virtually no common symbols now but flowers and candles.

It is no surprise either that many hymns, so much loved by older congregations and written in a period when much of the Christian story and symbolism were commonly known, are virtually incomprehensible these days. By contrast the language of some modern hymns, seeking to be more immediately appealing, can be reduced to the repetition of simple phrases: 'We just love you, Jesus'; 'Praise him, praise him, praise him'. They can feel a bit over-simplistic.

The church newcomer may have expected that not everything would be readily understood but some of it will feel unnecessarily obscure and inaccessible. There may be an aesthetic about the old and the quaint that appeals to some people and they may well be willing to stick with it to discover what the meanings are. But they will not be the majority. Most people will be more likely to say 'not again'.

Then there is the **sermon**! There are few places apart from church where people willingly sit through a monologue of 20, 30 or even 40 minutes. Apart from the occasional political speech, and these are often attended only by the party faithful (interesting phrase!), we do not receive our information, exhortation or learning in such large chunks. Education, including that of adults, seldom comes in the form of lectures with no interaction, participation or activity. We know that only a proportion of the population actually learns best through listening to another speak. There are those who learn mainly through what is visual or tactile. Some may be independent learners but most learn better when interacting with others. So while many churchgoers say that it is the sermon they really go for, something that feeds them, it is seldom this that proves attractive to the first-timer. Television producers know that a 'talking head' does not appeal if it goes on for very long. And for TV 'very long' means more than a couple of minutes. Our attention span is quite short these days. Messages have to be got across quickly – just look at adverts on TV. The message is built up of a series of images that individually often last for no more than about three seconds. Of course, sermons are meant to be doing something more complex than an advert but some of the lessons of the market place may be worth looking at. And in any case the public in the pew has usually already been shaped more than they imagine, or even want, by the methods of the media.

It could be argued that charismatic preaching overcomes all such obstacles. The great preachers and orators know how to hold an audience, how to move them, to stimulate thought and feelings, to stir and to enthuse. But such preachers aren't particularly thick on the ground. An all too common comment upon the sermon is: 'it's boring'.

The introduction of family worship, all-age worship and things like Messy Church have made inroads into the traditional sermon slot. Because young people are usually present on such occasions, efforts are made to stimulate their interest with stories, activities, puppets, pictures, DVDs and so on. The leaders of such worship can sometimes fear that they are making things too simple in appealing to children, but there are plenty of adults who happily sit through such sessions and lap it up. There are, of course, those who run a mile from such services – but then, as every church knows, you can't please everyone all the time.

The newcomer who finds herself at such a service may still not understand some of what is being referred to, may still feel awkward about any number of things, but will usually find it an occasion when people seem to be enjoying themselves and that can be attractive. Looking miserable has been the impression given by too many congregations coming out of a service. They may have been just thoughtful, they may have felt moved by the service and want time to reflect on it. But the perception is that they are miserable – and perceptions are powerful.

Much of what has been referred to in this chapter are experiences and perceptions at a fairly basic level. Any organisation or profession, club or institution has its own 'culture' and often its own language set. Step into a school staff meeting and anyone new to the world of education will soon find themselves out of their depth, bamboozled by jargon and acronyms. A golf club house can resound to conversations that leave a non-player in the dark and feeling out of it. Get astronomers talking about the latest discoveries and they might as well be aliens to those whose knowledge of science never got beyond the boiling point of water. So churches are not unique in presenting some problems for the person who first enters. What matters is what they do about it.

There is no point in blaming others. The vital thing is for churches to recognise that there is, in fact, a problem and that they need to do something about it. This is usually easier in the larger suburban and urban churches where there are more resources and it is possible to provide a range of services and styles of worship. Many churches are certainly making valiant efforts and there are examples of imaginative and creative work being done, not only to make churches themselves more accessible but to ensure that there is effective outreach into the community. But the overall picture remains concerning.

Is there a choice of worship for people to attend or is it all of one kind? BCP? All-age? Praise?

How accessible is the language of worship? Does it rely heavily on religious symbolism and story not in common usage or part of general knowledge?

THREE

'The way I see it ...'

As we have seen in the two previous chapters, there are plenty of reasons why people are put off going to church. Some of them are comparatively straightforward things like lack of comfort, old-fashioned language, or boring sermons. But even more powerful are the perceptions people have. Some may arise out of their own past experiences or reports of the experiences of others. They may be misconceptions or the result of half-knowledge. There may even be prejudices but for the person concerned they are real and it is no good church people just dismissing them.

'The way I see things' really matters and for many people it equates to the way things are. This may reflect a closed mind refusing to take on board wider information or different experiences, but not always. In a liberal society the view of the individual is actively encouraged and, at an extreme, one's own opinion is all that matters. As we shall see later, this presents some difficulties for a liberal society when it comes to the role of authority. Individuals are their own authority.

a. 'You don't have to go to church to be a good person.'

This appears to be self-evident. It would be a sign of religious bigotry to say that all the people who don't go to church are bad people. However, while churches may not put it as crudely as that, the way some of them talk about who is saved and who isn't ends up implying this. If the concept means anything to them at all, I guess most people would say that church people believe that it's the good who get saved and the rest don't. There is a broad acceptance that in some way going to church has some connection with being good. That may lead to the accusation of church people being hypocrites, but the link is clear. So stating that it is possible to be good without going to church is to affirm a belief in one's own basic goodness and a rejection of the churches' perceived definition of what counts as being good. The person may even be saying in a different way: 'I am going to be saved, whatever you may think.' The discussion at this level may, in fact, miss the crucial point that while 'goodness' may be a consequence of faith in Christ, it is not a prerequisite for God's love and forgiveness. Indeed, it was for sinners that Jesus said he had come (Matthew 9:13).

If asked what 'good' means, people will give a whole range of answers and many of them will be based on values that Christians could claim are derived from centuries of Christian teaching. We may no longer be a Christian country, if by that we mean that the majority of people are not Christians, but many of the prevailing values in society have certainly been shaped by the Christian faith. So when it comes to things like honesty, compassion, justice, kindness, and equality, it is difficult to say what is distinctively Christian and what isn't.

For most people being good would include being honest (at least most of the time), being kind (at least to most other people), insisting on justice (especially if it involves oneself) and championing other people's rights (so long as they don't infringe on one's own). Being good does make demands. It is certainly more than just wanting your own way on everything and always looking after number one. But it doesn't have to be too costly. After all, we're not perfect, and who wants to be trodden all over?

It is at this point that it begins to look as though there is a distinctiveness in the Christian understanding of 'good'. While goodness of itself may not be sufficient for salvation, the goodness of a Christian is not quite the same as simply that of a polite, caring, honest citizen. It has to include the implications of the 'goodness' seen in Jesus. At some point this will include self-giving love. But we have to be careful. It does the Christian cause no favours to imply that only Christians are self-giving. Church members don't have a monopoly on that kind of love. But, although the emphases are different, both the Catholic and the Protestant traditional views understand 'goodness' to be neither innate (it is the result of grace and the work of the Spirit) nor sufficient. Faith or trust in God has also to be somewhere in the mix.

This brief foray into theology is not intended to show that the non-church member is actually not good after all, but to indicate that when people say they are as good as those who go to church that may only be true in a particular way. Nor does it guarantee, of course, that churchgoers are actually good either. However, this does lead us to the next point.

b. 'You can be a perfectly good Christian without going to church.'
Once again there is a self-evident truth about this. In so far as we dare to judge who and who is not a 'good Christian', it does appear true that church-going itself is not the definitive activity. Churches may not like that. Indeed, some have insisted on church attendance as a requirement for membership, and even the state has legislated for it at various periods of history. The statistics quoted in the Introduction indicate that among those who consider themselves to be Christian, there is a significant proportion who do not attend church with any kind of regularity. Some would even consider that not going to church but walking in the countryside, for instance, helped them to worship God even more fully.

As we become an increasingly individualistic society, the practice of religion, the exercise of faith, and the exploration of spirituality tend to become more individualistic as well. There has long been a debate about the place of religion in the public scene, with the insistence by some that religion is essentially a private matter. In Christian teaching there is a balance which seeks to hold the individual and the corporate together. At one level there is the strong emphasis upon the total worth of every individual, based in the love of God for each one of us. But there is also a strong sense of the importance of relationships and the sense of being part of something bigger – the family, the tribe, the people of God (in the Old Testament) and the Body, the Church (in the New Testament). We are told that as a Christian on our own we are like a single burning coal, while together with others in worship and fellowship we are a blazing fire. There is plenty of teaching that says we develop in the faith by being part of a wider fellowship through whom we grow more fully in our knowledge and understanding of the faith and in our relationship with God.

The person who feels they can be a perfectly good Christian without going to church is not necessarily saying that a fellowship of faith and worship is not valuable for others. It just isn't for them. The church that either writes such people off by dismissing them from membership or harangues them for lack of commitment will certainly not encourage them to return nor help them in their spiritual journey.

Of course, it may all be a bit of an excuse for not doing what one doesn't want to do anyway. Putting the reason for not attending church in terms of being a Christian on one's own may simply be a way of avoiding the judgement of others, that by not going to church you are not, in fact, Christian. And for some people that still matters. After all, we don't particularly like being judged.

c. 'They're all so judgemental.'
John Wesley is often misquoted as having said: 'Catch on fire and others will love to come watch you burn.' The saying is, of course, not about self-immolation but about being on fire with the love of God, on fire with goodness (holiness). It conveys the belief that such a life is so appealing that others will want to witness it and, hopefully, copy it. True goodness can indeed be very attractive, especially – perhaps only – when it is unselfconscious. But there is also a 'goodness' which smacks of the self-righteous and which exudes a sense of judgement towards others: the colleague who never seems to make mistakes but hangs around just waiting to catch you out doing something not quite right, or the up-tight mother-in-law who knows how to bring up children perfectly and conveys an air of criticism whenever she visits.

This is the perception some people have of churchgoers and they have no intention of putting themselves in the way of that kind of criticism. In broad terms the perception may arise either from what the person has picked up generally about church attitudes, perhaps from the media, or from personal experience.

Churches can appear to be very judgemental. To some extent this is understandable. Religion is not only about beliefs but also behaviour. And most churches have rules and regulations about what people should and should not do. Salvationists, for example, are not allowed to smoke or drink. The appalling drunkenness of the Victorian working classes led to their members being encouraged to 'sign the pledge', and this still persists. These days, while alcohol continues to take its toll, not least with binge-drinking among the younger generation, and with drugs having become an even greater issue, it is sex that is seen as attracting most comment from the churches. In the popular mind it seems that the churches are obsessed with sex – or at least about all the things you shouldn't be doing sexually. Adultery is wrong – it's in the ten commandments – so is casual sex. Pornography is condemned. Gay sex has long been a focus of attention, controversy and attack.

In a liberal society where attitudes have changed rapidly over the last 70 years, many of the things condemned in the past both by the Church and by society generally are now tolerated. Thirty years ago, around two thirds of people in the United Kingdom were opposed to same-sex relationships; now it is only about one fifth. Half of the population agree in principle to gay marriage although it is still firmly opposed by most churches. In 1983 90% of people were against gay people being able to adopt children. By 2013 this had moved to 48%. Many churches do have a more tolerant attitude towards gay people than they once had, although it is often cloaked in terms of pastoral care rather than as a matter of principle. The approach that says gay orientation is acceptable but homosexual practices are wrong is still prevalent, and for the general public this is a bit of casuistry. It is just one of the many strands which build up the perception of judgemental churches.

The number of divorces rose considerably in the latter part of the twentieth century. In 1960 there were 23,868 divorces and by 1993 this had reached a peak of 165,018. The lower figure for 2012 of 118,140 reflects the changing patterns of marriage and the increase of 'living together in partnership'. In seeking to maintain the 'sanctity of marriage' churches have taken various degrees of hard line on the matter of divorce. In 2002 the General Synod of the Church of England passed this statement: 'The Church of England teaches that marriage is for life. It also recognises that sadly some marriages do fail and, if this should happen, it seeks to be available to all. The Church accepts that, in exceptional circumstances, a divorced person may marry again in church during the life-time of a former spouse.' It sounded as though a divorced person might be acceptable, but only in exceptional circumstances. And experience showed that it was not easy to prove one qualified as exceptional.

In the Roman Catholic Church, canon law makes no provision for divorce. The only way round it is to prove that the conditions of marriage were not properly met (e.g. consummation did not take place) and by legal process the marriage may be deemed never to have existed – it is null and void. The individuals concerned may then remarry in church. A person who has divorced and remarries in a civil ceremony is not allowed to receive communion:

> If the divorced are remarried civilly, they find themselves in a situation that objectively contravenes God's law. Consequently, they cannot receive Eucharistic communion as long as this situation persists. For the same reason, they cannot exercise certain ecclesial responsibilities. Reconciliation through the sacrament of Penance can be granted only to those who have repented for having violated the sign of the covenant and of fidelity to Christ, and who are committed to living in complete continence.'[4]

---

4. *Catechism of the Catholic Church, 1650.*

The Synod on the Family in Rome 2015 showed that, even among the bishops, there is no longer a single view on this or other significant matters around the nature of marriage, but the traditional position held sway.

Most conservative evangelical churches and other Protestant churches, like the Baptists, strongly oppose divorce and quote scripture in support of their view (e.g. Malachi 2:16).

The churches may well feel they have a strong case for taking the attitude they do, but to those on the outside it can feel off-putting and merely reinforce their perception of the Church.

The Race Relations Act of 1976 gave protection to people in the workplace against both direct and indirect discrimination by virtue of race. The legal system has attempted to 'outlaw' racism but that doesn't mean it has been eradicated from the minds, attitudes and behaviour of individuals and institutions. Urban churches have long had ethnic minority members but in rural areas the presence of black people is less obvious. Churches there will not refuse to allow a black person to join the worship but there are plenty of subtle and indirect ways by which a congregation or individuals can make it clear that they don't 'approve'. It can make it appear that to be black is to be judged as unacceptable. The same would be true for Travellers or tramps or hippies covered in tattoos, or for the disabled and those with cerebral palsy. The image of the suburban and village church is of congregations of 'conservative' white people who don't welcome those who are not like themselves – indeed, who judge them as not really acceptable. The perception may be false, based on no actual knowledge of how a particular church would react, but the perception is certainly around. There is enough evidence of racism within our society to know that the Church will not be immune.

d. 'They are such killjoys.'
A friend once said: 'I know I must be religious – I keep saying no to all the things I like doing.' It may be an exaggeration but religion has the reputation of being negative, especially about things most people see as fun – drink, sex, gambling, just having a good time. There is within

most religions an element of asceticism. Such things as the monastic tradition of chastity, poverty and obedience, the encouragement to 'give up something for Lent' and sermons against the 'sins of the flesh' have somehow spread the assumption into the atmosphere that, in order to please God, people have to give up lots of things they would normally enjoy. God, it seems to many, is like the parent who tells a child to go and find her brother and tell him to stop whatever he is doing. It doesn't help that the Ten Commandments are rather heavy on 'Thou shalt not'.

e. 'They're just a load of hypocrites.'

There is a perception that churchgoers think they are better than everyone else. It may not be clear how the perception has arisen and may not, in fact, relate to anyone in particular. It's a view that is just out there, and in the pub or at a dinner party it's the kind of thing that gets said as a fact and usually gets a broad nod of agreement. Ask if Mrs Jennings, the one who arranges the flowers in the church, or Kevin Phillips, who plays the organ, are hypocrites and as likely as not everyone agrees they don't mean them. But it remains a well-known fact that churchgoers are hypocrites, and that they act all 'holy' while in fact they are no better than the rest of us.

Underpinning this perception is the idea that churchgoers *ought* to be better than the rest of us and that that is what religion is really about. It assumes that religion is primarily about behaviour rather than belief. To many Christians the perception that they are hypocrites may well appear very unfair. They would certainly agree that they try to behave as well as they can and live decent lives, but not that they claim to be perfect or necessarily better than everyone else. The press only has to run a story about naughty vicars going to a strip club, or Sunday school teachers having an affair with a choir member and everyone feels their view about church people being hypocrites is justified. And of course such stories don't help. The fact that most churchgoers recognise that they are forgiven sinners rather than spotless saints makes little impact upon the way they may be perceived.

As petty or serious as these complaints are, they focus on individuals and generalisations are made from that. But sometimes it is the whole institution of the Church that is seen to be hypocritical. The Church Commissioners play a key role in the finances of the Church of England. Every now and then the press runs stories about the way they manage their investments or their property estate. Although they are very careful to maintain an ethical investment policy, they are occasionally found to have invested in a company one of whose subsidiaries is involved in arms manufacture or in clothes factories that employ child labour. This leads to disinvestment, but in the public mind it is yet another example of the 'church' being hypocritical.

The abuse of children and young adults is an even more serious matter and over the past few years churches have rightly come under scrutiny. That clergy, bishops even, should have perpetrated such actions is appalling but that the Church should have attempted to hush it up out of embarrassment makes a bad situation worse. People are rightly critical and the reputation of the Church is severely damaged. Both the Roman Catholic Church and the Church of England have been guilty here.

f. 'It's all rules and regulations.'
Organisations have to have rules: rules of membership, rules of the conduct of business, rules about financial arrangements. There cannot be a free-for-all. But rules can be a pain, especially when they appear to be unnecessary, overcomplicated and out of date. Churches talk a lot about being welcoming and claim that their own welcome is based upon God's unconditional love and invitation. But that is not how it always appears to the person who approaches the church with a specific request.

Consider Betty Hargreaves. She and her husband, Joe, used to enjoy an evening at their favourite pub by the church in the village next to the one where they lived. When Joe died, Betty wanted him to be buried in the churchyard just over the wall from their favourite pub, where they had spent so many happy times. She thought it would be straightforward. There was still plenty of room and she had decided on a nice headstone. But things were not that simple.

Their house in the neighbouring village wasn't in the same parish and they had not booked a grave space. The vicar was sorry but said these were the rules. She suggested Betty went to the vicar in her own parish. Somewhat reluctantly, Betty did so and it was arranged for Joe to be buried in the churchyard in their own village. She then hit a problem over the headstone she had chosen. It was a dark, shiny granite with gold lettering and she wanted it to say 'Joe Hargreaves – a good old boy'. The Vicar explained that it didn't comply with the rules and the fact that there was one just like it in the local cemetery made no difference. Explanations about traditional churchyards and suitable memorials, faculties and Chancellor's regulations left Betty feeling angry and hurt. She hasn't been near the church since. As she told her neighbour – 'all they worry about is their petty rules'. That may be harsh, unfair even, but that's how she saw it.

Her neighbour Joyce sympathised and they tut-tutted together as Joyce explained the fuss her daughter had had over wanting her baby christened in a pretty little church only five miles from the town where she lived. They'd had to see the rector there a couple of times, fill in forms, then go and see their own local vicar, who they'd never met before, to 'get his permission'. And after all that, they had to attend a couple of sessions at the vicarage along with some other couples having their babies 'done' and there was a great fuss about their choice of godparents. It seems one of them hadn't been baptised and 'is that the same as christened?'. 'It's no wonder churches are empty,' Joyce concluded.

As the established Church with its long history, it is not particularly surprising that the Church of England has a fair number of rules, none of which are likely to be known by the general public. Attempts have been made to relax some of the requirements – as, for example, with the level of connection a couple has to have with a church where they wish to get married. But even then the regulations are still fairly restrictive – not only because of what the Church says but because weddings in churches are covered by the secular law as well. The perception, however, is that it is the Church that makes life difficult for people. The generalisation builds from particular experiences shared and discussed, not always with knowledge of all the facts.

g. 'They're always after your money.'

There are countries where the churches receive support from the state, in some cases towards general expenses, elsewhere specifically with the cost of the church buildings. While there are limited grants in the United Kingdom for the maintenance of some church buildings, there is no state support towards general expenses. Churches are charities and are maintained either through historical assets, through the generosity of the membership or through fundraising – or a combination of all three. It is a well-known complaint by members of local church 'governing' bodies (councils or committees) that too much time is spent discussing finances. Congregations can get fundraising-weary and the appeals for church funds, tower repairs or a new heating system can seem endless. Go into church and as often as not at some point a collection will be taken or there will be a plate strategically placed at the back by the door as you leave. Many cathedrals charge to go in.

The criticism that churches are always wanting money is most likely to be aimed at the more traditional churches, especially the Church of England. It's less likely to be directed against the independent and evangelical churches, in part because their members are generally more generous in giving to the church, often maintaining the ancient tradition of tithing, and this makes appeals for money less obvious. The Salvation Army will rattle tins in shopping precincts or wherever its bands play but it's not perceived to be rich and is known for doing a lot of good for the poor and homeless. There is a lot of sympathy for what they do. But the CofE and the Roman Catholic Church are perceived to be wealthy. It's partly the size and number of their buildings – just think of those cathedrals, the big houses the clergy live in, bishops' palaces and all that. You only have to go into one of their churches and they've got silver this and gold that. And just think of all the land that the CofE is said to own. They're swimming in it. That is the perception and the outstretched hand of the Church makes it look as though it is always asking for more. For some people that's a put-off.

h. 'It's just full of old women.'

One shouldn't despise elderly women, of course. The Orthodox Church in Russia survived largely through the faithfulness of older women. But for young people and young families, a church where the average age of the congregation is knocking on 70 is not particularly appealing. We saw earlier that the Methodist Church is concerned about the ageing demographic of its members and a report from the Church of England in 2014 showed that the average age of its members was 62 with nearly half of its congregations having fewer than five members under the age of 16.

There is some truth in the perception that there are more women than men in church, although they are not necessarily all old. A Tearfund report in 2013 indicated that in UK churches only 35% of those who attend are men. What is surprising is that this is a figure similar to that indicated by a survey of congregations in London in 1904! People like to give explanations of why there is this imbalance. Some say it is because women are innately more religious – but that is not borne out by some religions other than Christianity. Has the rise of feminism, the increasing number of women priests, the changing role of women in society contributed to the lack of men in church? Each has certainly been suggested. It is also claimed that church – and by that is meant its message, its ethos, its activity – is just more appealing to women. Men look for masculinity, risk and challenge and they don't see those in church. The very things the Church emphasises, like love and compassion, are perceived as 'soft' qualities more appropriate for women. The trouble is that some of the explanations appear to stereotype men and women as well as the Church and that will do little to help find a solution to the imbalance of gender in so many churches.

Nearly every church I have ever known bewails the fact that it can't attract enough youngsters and young couples. Sometimes there just isn't anyone, including the minister, who is really good at leading all-age or family worship. But when something new is tried in the hope of attracting younger people, it does not help if all the regulars stay at home just because it's not going to be 'Matins'!

i. 'They can't even agree with one another.'

There have been differences and splits in the Christian Church from the beginning, as is evident from the Letters of St Paul. And it has always been felt that this is not how it should be. In his account of the Last Supper, John records Jesus praying for the unity of his followers (John 17:11). The disunity of the Church is evident both locally and globally. There is the split between Orthodox and Catholic and Protestant, and divisions within each of them. Some Churches are worldwide, others as local as a single congregation. A person looking up 'churches' in a local directory is presented with a whole list. The division is there for all to see – and criticise. For many Christians too it is the great scandal – one of the many blocks that put people off.

Within churches division is also obvious. In the Catholic Church, as elsewhere, there is the division between the traditionalists and the reformers. There are those who still want the Latin Mass while others insist on the Mass being in the local language. Among others there are calls for women to be ordained and the end to the requirement for all clergy to be celibate. Anglicans form a worldwide Communion of some 85 million members. They speak of the Anglican family, yet it is a family that is in grave danger of splitting up over the issue of homosexuality. There are divisions over doctrine, divisions over liturgy, divisions over ethics, divisions over authority, divisions over the interpretation of the scriptures. Appeals for Christians to focus on what all have in common too often disclose that what is really held in common is rather limited.

There have been visionary leaders who have struggled to bring Christians together. The efforts of Nathan Söderblom, Archbishop of Uppsala, and of George Bell, Bishop of Chichester, among others, led to the formation of the World Council of Churches in 1948. The week of Prayer for Christian Unity is observed by many churches each January. Since 1971 unions have brought together the Presbyterian and Congregational Churches. In 2003, after decades of conversation, the Anglican and Methodist Churches signed a Covenant. In some places, churches of different denominations come together in ecumenical arrangements, sharing church buildings and worship. Relationships between churches are often cordial. The exceptions make the headlines and underline the perception that Christians just can't agree among themselves yet seem to be constantly making calls for others to find a way through their own particular disagreements.

Even a cursory glance at history reveals just how deep, tragic and bloody the division between Christians has been, each side convinced that they alone have the truth and killing those who disagree with them. Battles have been fought, torture chambers filled and fires lit in the belief that they are needed to save the faith from heresy and that through them the true religion of a God of love can be maintained.

j. 'It's so old-fashioned and out of date.'

This is often said by people whose knowledge of the Church is limited to what things were like when they were young some 40 years ago when they were taken to church and were bored. Without always knowing the ways many churches have changed, it is assumed they are all still like it was 30, 80, 200 years ago. And in some instances they may be right. Look at the way the clergy dress up for a start, all black cassocks and dog collars and things that look like night shirts and fancy cloaks. OK for a bit of nostalgia and pantomime, but what has that got to do with where the world is today? Clergy ought to be people you can approach easily if you want to and this just distances them. There are plenty of the younger clergy and ministers who would agree and they abandon the traditional clergy garb. Unfortunately, this is just as likely to receive complaints that jumpers and jeans make them look just like anyone else and lack a proper sense of reverence. You can't win.

My curate and I had different views on such matters, especially when it came to visits to the local pubs, fruitful places for outreach and pastoral care (we claimed). He never wore a dog collar. I always did. His view was that people were put off and wouldn't approach him if he had a dog collar on. People saw him as more like them and felt more at ease. He had a point, but my view was that there were also those who didn't want us to be just one of them, and that those who didn't know I was a priest and started chatting with me could be taken aback and feel cheated when it became clear I was the local vicar. We each did our own thing and that was fine.

Not all churches adopted the cassock and surplice, cotta and chasuble fashions, but gowns of various colours along with 'preaching tabs' have been common. Similar to academic gowns, they gave the aura of authority and learning. In many places, but by no means all, these too have been abandoned as old-fashioned.

Clergy and ministers have long been referred to as 'the Reverend'. While church people hardly think about it, such a title can appear to the 'outsider' as old-fashioned and rather pretentious. It is even worse when going up the hierarchy: Venerable, Very Reverend, Right Reverend, Most Reverend. Although it is not common, bishops can still get addressed as 'my Lord'. One delightful elderly and rather traditional priest I knew was once heard to address the new suffragan bishop as 'my Lord'. When the bishop told him 'Bishop' was quite sufficient, the priest explained that, as someone who stammered, 'my Lord' was much easier than 'b-b-b-bishop'. All this can seem quite harmless, a kind of ecclesiastical eccentricity built into the traditions of the Church – just the Church's way of differentiating offices of different rank. But in an egalitarian society it can rankle as well as confuse.

To those not in the know it's a mystery why some clergy are called priests or presbyters, others pastors, others ministers, some deans, some canons. Then there are vicars and rectors, curates and deacons, provosts and archdeacons, superintendents and district chairmen, rural deans, urban deans, area deans, vicars general and cardinals, suffragan bishops, area bishops and diocesan bishops. No wonder people are frightened to address clergy in case they get it wrong.

More serious are the perceptions that the Church lives in a world long gone, a world of afternoon tea and cucumber sandwiches, flannel graphs and children's corners. It's a world where 'wealth creation' is a dirty word and management something best left to business and commerce. A world of outdated morals and a culture that has little contact with or understanding of today's youth culture. A guitar-playing vicar strumming the odd song from the 1960s is not exactly 'with it' (or whatever the latest equivalent phrase is). Unfair? Of course it is. Totally untrue? Sadly not.

In a time of rapid change, 'old-fashioned' is largely felt to be the equivalent of 'irrelevant'. Faith, churchgoing, Christian values that for a time and for many people were the foundation of their lives and the life of the nation are all being eroded. For increasing numbers it seems that the Christian God is either dead or of no immediate relevance. Other value systems have taken the place of traditional religion. Explanations of how the universe ticks are not looked for in theology books or from sermons but in the language of mathematics and the research of scientists. The old authorities have lost their power and there is suspicion of authority in general. You can get on perfectly well, it is claimed, without any reference to God or without ever entering a church. In fact some would say you are better off if you have nothing to do with either.

It is to these wider issues that we will now turn. But first, a brief word to add a note of cheer to what so far may have seemed rather gloomy.

FOUR

It's Not All Doom and Gloom

It is inevitable that a book dealing with some of the reasons for the reluctance of people to go to church and for the decline in numbers attending church is selective and has a negative feel. Statistics, if at all reliable, necessarily deal with big numbers. They give an overall picture for populations and large groups. Surveys deal with thousands of people. The more people that are surveyed, the more likely it is that the survey will be accurate. But they cannot be guaranteed to identify what is true for a particular individual. For example, statistics show that smoking is the most frequent cause of preventable death. A study in America reported that men who smoke have about half the chance of reaching the age of 73 compared to non-smokers. But if you ask Chuck Smith, who has smoked 20 cigarettes a day since he was 12, how old he is, he will tell you 94, although his brother who never smoked died when he was 58!

As we have seen, the general picture of church decline needs to be countered by the fact that in some places and with some churches there is growth. For every generalisation made about old, cold, damp, uncomfortable buildings, it is possible to find examples where this is not the case and where even a medieval church has been reordered in an imaginative and inviting way, offering warmth, comfort, flexibility ... and loos. So it is important that what has been written here is kept in proportion. Constant talk of decline can become a self-fulfilling prophecy by undermining the confidence and vitality of a church. The picture is always more complex. In the Church of England, for example, there are gloomy predictions that, unless the current number of ordinands increases by 50%, there will be about half the present number of clergy by 2020. What looks depressing can also be seen as a challenge. In fact, not only is the number of ordinands increasing but, more significantly, the percentage of those under 31 years of age has increased in the last five years from 15% to 25%. So it's not all bad news.

Realism rather than pessimism is what is required. The intention is to acknowledge that there is general decline, to look at the possible reasons realistically, even when they arise from mistaken or ill-informed perceptions, and to consider what might be done about it.

There is a challenge here. To every situation there is a range of possible reactions: 'let's ignore it'; 'it's only a passing phase'; 'so we have a problem – let's deal with it'; 'they should have done something about it'; 'God's in charge – he'll sort it out'. In some situations there are just not the resources to make major changes. Some people find it easier to blame others than to take responsibility themselves. Out of crisis a leader can unexpectedly arise but sometimes there just doesn't seem to be anyone. Whatever the difficulty, it is not true to say that nothing can be done. It's a matter of identifying which aspect can be tackled with the resources available, clarifying what the overall aim is, and then having a go, not biting off more than can be chewed. Not every effort will succeed, but with no effort there will not be any success.

We have looked at some of the issues that a local church may well feel they could do something about – not all at once perhaps, but bit by bit. The problems may be considerable but are potentially manageable. They are largely particular and local in scope– a pew to be removed here, a change of attitude there, a new form of service once a month, a list of visitors drawn up, a new hymn book introduced. But there are wider matters that can feel less tangible, more intractable. They arise from past history or current social patterns, they are embedded in ingrained attitudes or even in the way human beings are made. Large social trends are more difficult to get your head round and to know how you can influence them. But they are worth considering because they put the local difficulties into a broader context and, hopefully, will take away some of the guilt that can weigh heavily on churchgoers when they cannot attract more people to church. That's what will be considered next.

In the following section of the book, the perspective changes. An attempt will be made to draw out some of the 'big' issues and then go on to see what it is in the Christian faith that might hold the key to finding some answers. So there are some positives to look forward to!

PART TWO

FIVE

The Economic Context

In the 1980s and 1990s my brother-in-law was Vicar of St Martin-in-the Fields in London. The church had, and continues to have, a worldwide reputation for its work with the homeless and poor, the troubled and the addicted through its social care centre. It is a church famous for its services broadcast on the BBC. Over the decades it has had a succession of able and saintly clergy, including Dick Sheppard and Austen Williams. When my brother-in-law became vicar he found the church was in a financial crisis. It had failed to recognise that to do all the marvellous work it was involved in required sustainable financial resources. To turn things round and create a sound financial basis required vision, courage and a change of attitude to wealth and wealth creation. To put it crudely, the church had to catch up with the times and recognise the realities of living in a capitalist system.

Traditionally, Christianity has been suspicious of wealth, even though some churches have been very wealthy (part of its hypocrisy?). The rich, Jesus told his followers, had as much chance of getting into heaven as a fully loaded camel getting through the eye of a needle (possibly a reference to a narrow city gate into Jerusalem). The love of money is said to be the root of all evil. The rich do not get a good press in Jesus' parables. Sermons aplenty have been preached against the accumulation of wealth, about wicked financiers and the corrupt capitalist system.

Yet in reality, since the collapse of communism, capitalism is the only game in town. It is the global economic system – and we all benefit, or suffer, because of it. In subtle ways that we are largely unconscious of, it influences our beliefs and our behaviour.

One of the things that capitalism grew out of and encouraged was a change of vision about the future. Before the rise of capitalism (and that covers many millennia), the future, if it was thought about at all, was largely a place of threat rather than promise. The possibility of a steadily improving prospect for human well-being was unknown. If anything, the future was more likely to be a time of general deterioration. The only hope was for there to be a transformation. It would be cataclysmic but nothing less would do. And only God could do it. He would have to change things round in a power play. The present would not grow gradually into a better future but there would have to be a new creation – a new heaven and a new earth. The thought of progress through human endeavour was hardly entertained.

This went along with a view that the wealth of the world was more or less fixed. The goodies cake was only so big and didn't grow. So if *you* got a big slice, *I* had to go short. If I got more of the cake, someone else would by necessity have to have less. So being rich was ethically questionable – it meant someone had inevitably been made poorer. The growth of capitalism changed this, so that it became morally desirable to be a wealth creator because, at its best, the wealthy ploughed their wealth back into productivity which had a general benefit – more employment, more goodies at cheaper prices. Wealth was no longer seen as a fixed amount. The cake could grow. Growth became the watchword and the driving force of economics. That at least was how Adam Smith explained it in his 1776 seminal book, *The Wealth of Nations*.

Capitalism is actually built on smoke and mirrors. It works very well so long as everyone trusts that it works. This is reflected in such phrases as 'My word is my bond' and the promise made on every British bank note by the Chief Cashier of the Bank of England. Undermine that trust and the system is in trouble, as was all too obvious in the financial crisis of 2008 and may occur again with the slow-down of the Chinese economy. Global economics sound hard-nosed and objective but depend on something less tangible: faith – faith that human ingenuity and inventiveness can continually come up with new products and production methods, new sources of energy and greater energy efficiency, and new raw materials to create the new products, and can convince everyone they need an ever-increasing number of things – more stuff, the latest gizmo, the newest model. If human beings come up with all of this, capitalism not only succeeds, it will continue. Lack these things and it is undermined and the whole world will be in a mess. Even these things are not enough. Along with trust there has to go a level of altruism – those with wealth have to invest their wealth into more production, not simply spend it all on opulence for themselves. And there has to be a general level of honest dealing. Because human beings are too often given to corruption and double-dealing, there has to be regulation. If ethics don't work, the law has to step in. And the history of capitalist venture has shown that, left to themselves, the wealth creators all too easily become exploitative, manipulative, self-seeking. The Dutch merchants and joint stockholders did this in Indonesia, the British in India.

For good or bad, we all live in a capitalist world and it affects the way we think and the way we behave. At its worst it makes individuals into production units where efficiency and low costs override any consideration of personal well-being or worth. It led to the slave trade – a trade that was blessed and run as well as eventually 'abolished' through Christian leadership. One of the criticisms of the traditional churches is that they encouraged slavery, and people do not want to be identified with institutions that did that. At its best capitalism leads to an increasing-sized cake of goodies and general improvement in the standard of living of everyone. In reality, it may be a global system but it has yet to create an equal world – just look at the number of economic migrants seeking to leave poverty and move to a better life.

To be effective it has also had to turn us all into consumers. Economic growth needs people to buy more and more stuff. When national economies suffer recession, everyone is encouraged to buy more things to kick-start the recovery. 'Stop saving for the rainy days, the sun will shine if you spend.' It just depends on trust, hope, promise and credit, and us all playing our part as consumers.

As consumers, we have been encouraged (brainwashed?) to want things now. Shopping is good for us. If you feel down, try some retail therapy. It seems we should not only spend our way out of recession but also out of depression! There is an impatience about consumers. Credit 'takes the waiting out of wanting'. As canny consumers, we can put a price on anything and we want value for money. So was the service I have just attended worth the money I put in the collection? Is a church worth forking out for to keep it standing? What's in it for me? There's the possibility that I could spend my money more effectively to get my spiritual nourishment – buy a yoga video, for instance. And in any case going to church will get in the way of the visit to the shopping mall. Sunday's the one time we can get out as a family and buy stuff.

Most religions encourage forms of asceticism among their followers. Indeed, it could be said to be fundamental to Buddhism where adherents aim to overcome their 'cravings' which the Buddha identified as the root cause for all anxiety, pain and suffering. The Shakers of America had a similar outlook. So whether it be for particular days or times of the day, most religions advocate abstaining from all or some foods (Advent, Lent and Fridays for Christianity, fasting during festivals in Hinduism, the month of Ramadan in Islam, Yom Kippur and Tisha B'Av in Judaism). Priests in these religions may be asked to undergo greater fasts and abstinence in regard to other 'cravings', such as sex. Such fasting has the purpose of enhancing the spiritual life. Consumerism has no desire to inhibit 'cravings' – indeed, it encourages them, even depends upon them. Since 'cravings' (*the desires of the flesh*) are common to human nature's 'default' position, consumerism is in this sense running with the grain of our basic human nature. Religion goes against the grain, seeking to discipline, control or eliminate such cravings. Little wonder then that consumerism has an easier time in its desire to influence our behaviour and attitudes – it goes along with our wishes, doesn't ask us to rein them in. It's natural to want things, so why go against nature?

In spite of all the guidance of the wise men and women down the ages, our consumerist society has managed to convince itself that happiness can be bought or that at least it will be discovered in the next purchase even if it didn't quite come along with this one. Happiness, the United States constitution tells us, is a right and in case we should look in the wrong place for it, the capitalist system points us to possessions. Despite the fact that we soon discover that just having things doesn't ensure happiness, we persist in the search online, in shops, at retail outlets. What in fact is happening is a 'shallowing' of what we mean by happiness and it is increasingly linked with individualism – my right to be happy, in my way. That happiness could mean denying myself for the sake of others looks increasingly like the outlook of killjoys and that's what religious people are – happiness stoppers. Unfair? Of course, but there's enough power in this consumerist fantasy for it to be unwise for churches to ignore it or simply rail against it. For a complex of reasons, our being 'selfish', 'self-focused' or 'self-centred' seems to be increasingly acceptable – even something to defend. No wonder people feel judged when they go to church and hear how wicked it is to be selfish. The Church seems to be just getting at them, and who wants to be made to feel that uncomfortable?

Going to church is, of course, intended to be much more than just a social event, a chance to meet friends, have a chat, socialise. But we would be very foolish to ignore this aspect. The lack of some degree of socialising is one of the reasons congregations in rural areas are so unhappy when the vicar rushes in to take the service and then rushes off to get to the service in the next church. But consumerism and the shopping experience have their social aspect and for some people this meets a need that church once did. A visit to the garden centre may actually be the one time in the week the family all get together. Supermarkets have cafés in them. Friends meet up to exchange news about good offers and latest purchases. This may be truer of women than men, but then churches have traditionally also attracted more women than men.

That is putting it all rather crudely, but if churches do not understand something of the power of the consumer culture and its influence upon behaviour and attitudes, they will find themselves more and more out on a limb, irrelevant. The capitalist system could be seen as a kind of alternative religious system in which money is worshipped, the tower block headquarters of banks and business become its cathedrals, the chief executives and investment gurus are its priests and everyone is called to be regularly involved in its activities. Is it not the new idolatry?

A system that depends heavily on faith and trust might well be felt to be operating in a similar landscape to that of religion. To some extent that makes it all the more dangerous. The two are operating in overlapping territories and the attraction of the one can be viewed as a threat to the other. 'You cannot serve God and mammon!' (Matthew 6:24; Luke 16:13). While to some, capitalism could be seen as a 'godsend', to others it might be viewed as 'the work of the devil'. But at the most it is a pseudo religion – it is a human product and, whatever its most ardent supporters might say, it was not worked out under the dictate of God or even a god. It has produced and been the product of human ingenuity and inventiveness. The progress it has made possible has been as a result of human endeavour. The rise of capitalism, along with the Enlightenment, the Industrial Revolution and the scientific age, have shown just how clever human beings are. They don't require divine intervention to account for their achievements. All this has produced a shift in the sense of dependency, away from God. Humanity is more self-confidently self-reliant and God becomes increasingly redundant. Death, of course, reveals an obvious limit to human ability and this puts increasing pressure on the medical profession to both extend life and prevent death. At the same time there are moves to legalise assisted dying (euthanasia) which can also be seen as a way for humans to take control in an area previously the prerogative of God. We are in charge and can manage very well.

Except when things go wrong, as they inevitably do. The system produces its exploiters, its corrupt practices, its greed and its bad faith. That the human spirit is capable of evil is all too evident. The question is what to do about it. And a system that is focused on human activity has to seek human answers. In recent years it has been the banks that have come in for particular attention. The lack of an agreed ethic produced behaviour that regulation has had to deal with. Bank executives saying sorry has not been enough. Enormous fines have been imposed. Trust had been eroded. But the system has survived and recovery has merely proved to many people that human beings can bounce back, get over things.

There may well have been plenty of people who suddenly turned to prayer as their finances hit a crisis but, as important as it is that churches are available to people in times of crisis, there must be more to religion than being a last-ditch ambulance service or insurance policy. These very notions have, in fact, been the basis of much criticism of religion: that it is merely a plaster on our bruises, a comforting consolation amidst loss, but has little to say to those who are strong or successful or confident or in times of well-being. If religion does not deal with the hard realities of life – sin, illness, guilt, death – it could be seen as mere tinsel, but if it is not relevant to the good, the achievements and the joy of life, it can be seen as failing to meet where many people feel themselves to be. Religion has to be a way of celebration and a means of a full life but also a way of facing and dealing with loss, pain and suffering. The big questions of meaning, evil, success and suffering remain and these have traditionally been religion's territory. They still are, but more and more people seek to answer these questions without bringing God into it. Indeed, for many, God merely adds to the problem.

A survey from the Marriage Foundation (November 2014) indicated that more 'middle and upper wealth' couples are likely to marry than those who are poorer. One commentator, not very helpfully, concluded that this showed that wealthier people are more moral! A more feasible conclusion could be that there is a greater financial benefit to the wealthier if they get married. Given the current legislation regarding marriage as against living together, marriage is one way for a couple to protect their money and to deal with it in a tax-efficient way. If you don't have money, these things aren't relevant! We might also note that there seems to be more emphasis these days put on the wedding than on the marriage. *Brides* magazine estimated that in 2014 the average cost of a wedding was almost £24,000. That is quite a disincentive for poorer people to get married. Of course weddings don't need to cost anywhere near that amount, but a wedding has become a matter of 'putting on a good show' and that means a show as good as one's peers. Couples wait years to get married, not to be certain they are marrying the right person but to save for the wedding. And if money is short, the wedding is put off. It's a consumerist matter, not one of marital ethics. Churches may be dismayed that this is the case but they need to understand it and take it into account, not simply hold up their hands in horror.

The capitalist/consumerist environment is just one of the major influences upon our beliefs, attitudes and behaviour that should be taken into account when we look for reasons why churchgoing and organised religion have declined. In broad terms we have identified a number of factors which play their part in creating a modern 'mind-set':

a. belief in a future where progress is in human hands

b. an ethic where having possessions/wealth is a positive

c. a recognition of the need for regulation to control the system from human error and malpractice

d. trust in a system rather than through personal relationship

e. the purchasing power of money to enhance a sense of worth and individual happiness

f. money is impersonal – 'my money is as good as yours', and 'I am as good as you'

g. consumerism encourages natural 'cravings'.

SIX

The Scientific Outlook

In March 2015 the Templeton World Charity Foundation and Durham University announced a three-year project that would bring together scientists, theologians and church leaders to promote greater understanding of the relationship between science and faith.[5] The programme is led by Professor David Wilkinson from the Department of Theology and Religion, Professor Tom McLeish from the Department of Physics, and Richard Cheetham, Bishop of Kingston. In commenting upon the programme, each referred to the conflict that still exists between science and theology and the fear and misconceptions some church leaders and many church members have about science.

We may be a long way from the kind of antagonism that Darwin and his followers experienced when they suggested that human beings are not a discrete creation but evolved from apes. Nevertheless, there remain those who regard the Genesis story as the final word on the way the universe and our world came into existence and who consider the scientific explanation as a fraud. One only has to look at some conservative evangelical websites or consider the controversy (not always well informed) about academies established by bodies who espouse creationism. The Bible may claim that creation was the result of a 'Word'

---

5. See http://www.templetonworldcharity.org/projects/equipping-church-leadership-age-of-science.

being spoken (God said and it was so), but the scientific approach is based on mathematics, not words, and for many mathematics wins out.

What is often at stake is the question of authority – the authority of the scriptures and the authority of science. Whenever there appears to be a conflict, the general public opt for science and the biblical literalists opt for Scripture. Each is taking a particular view, whether consciously or not, about the nature of the Bible. Each assumes that, among whatever else it may be about, it sets itself up (in the Book of Genesis) to be an account of creation and the nature of the physical world, comparable to that offered by science. This is not the only way of interpreting the Bible, of course, but the alternatives have a degree of subtlety about them that some people aren't prepared to explore. It's a lot simpler to take a straightforward stand – either science is right or the Bible is right. It is believed (itself an interesting word in this context) that science is fact, that it explains how things really are, while the Bible is myth, by which is meant fantasy. There is a danger that this attitude to the Bible, arising from both extreme scepticism and extreme acceptance, will spill over into wider issues about the relationship between science and religion and lead to a suspicion that the churches as 'holders' of religion are out of touch with where most people stand.

So there is still much work to be done, not only to help science and church leaders to work out a more positive relationship, but to help that relationship filter down into society in general. As Bishop Richard has said, 'The prevailing idea that the two are in conflict is remarkably persistent despite the vast amount of excellent academic literature giving a different view.' But of course there's the rub: what goes on in the academic world can take a long time to percolate through. The occasional dramatic headline has its effect but the relationship between science and religion is more subtle and complex than the headlines indicate. For all too many people, religion is considered to be incompatible with science – just think of all that creation, miracles, interfering God stuff. It is assumed that scientists really *know* about things, while religious people only *believe* they know.

It can be claimed, however, that this assumption needs to be turned on its head to understand what really drives the difference between religion and science. Put very simply, science advances in knowledge of the ways things are – the facts – by having the humility to understand that it is ignorant. Religion, which largely deals with mysteries rather than facts, has the presumption to think it knows the answers already. Science hypothesises. Religion dogmatises. The Christian religion, for example, formulated its foundational way of describing God and Christ 1700 years ago and congregations repeat the formula every week, with every new member, every priest, being required to subscribe to it. Scientists know that on average a scientific 'fact' has a very short 'shelf-life', possibly as short as 25 years. Science advances by constantly changing its opinion, its definitions, its understanding. Religion sustains itself through conserving its past insights. Intuitively we might think that a system that investigates the way things really are and which keeps changing its mind would have little authority and little credibility, while one that lives by a solid reliance on long-established statements would be seen as dependable and authoritative. But it doesn't work out like that. The way society largely views things actually acts counter-intuitively, and for many people the scientific way is what they take to be the best way to know what things are and how things work.

In terms of the whole history of humankind, the scientific approach is a newcomer. In any sustainable and general way, it has only been around for about 500 years. The religious approach had dominated for millennia. But for much of the time today and for a great many people, it is the scientific outlook that dominates. It is taken for granted. Observation, measurement and analysis are the methods of those who use this approach. The rest is speculation, and the thing to do with speculation is to bring observation, measurement and analysis to bear upon it; if it doesn't stand up to this, it is best to ditch speculation's conclusions. You cannot weigh a soul, so, it is argued, to postulate that people have souls is mistaken. You might not be able to measure beauty, but you can investigate the neurological events that occur when someone sees or hears something they describe as beautiful. For the positivist scientific approach, that is all there is to it.

The fact that we are actually living in a post-positivist world hasn't really caught on yet in the minds of the general public. Investigations of subatomic matter, where there are inbuilt levels of uncertainty, have led some scientists to postulate the possibility of 'external', even 'divine', intervention into events, but that kind of idea has not yet encroached on most of our thinking. There is a general, if somewhat simple, view of what science is about and tells us, and for plenty of people it doesn't leave room for God, let alone for such notions as God becoming man, the efficacy of prayer, resurrection, walking on water – the stuff of so much that is said, heard and sung about in church. What goes on in church is based on the 'incredible', not on the 'believable'.

For much of the time this conflict between science and religion is not uppermost in people's minds and for some it is no longer a conflict. Dr John Polkinghorne is a theoretical physicist, who resigned his post as Professor of Mathematical Physics at Cambridge University in order to be ordained as a priest in the Church of England. He has written a number of books in which he has sought to show the way in which science and theology can be reconciled. Dr Richard Cheetham, as a bishop, is seeking to do the same from the Church's standpoint. Each is well versed in the academic world and the language of both science and theology. And there are plenty of other people who have come to a position in which they can hold the two approaches, the religious and the scientific, in a reasonable state of complementarity. In doing so, they see the religious and scientific quests as setting out not only with different assumptions but with different questions. Put simply, they see religion as being primarily interested in 'Why?' and 'Who?' while the scientists are more concerned about 'How?' and 'What?' That the exploration of these different questions produces not only different answers but different styles of answer is not seen as a reason for opting for one set over against the other, but for holding them together and so gaining a richer insight. That there are 'pinch points' is accepted and they are the stimulus for further discussion.

The majority of people, including those who are religious, happily take on the practical outcomes of scientific research, not least in the worlds of medicine and information technology. Some church people do hold out against such advances. Perhaps most famously there are the Amish communities in America, amongst whom there are restrictions on the use of such things as electricity, telephones and cars. Members of some strict Pentecostal churches refuse to have televisions or to allow their children to go to the cinema, while blood transfusions are viewed with suspicion by some Christians. But members of mainstream churches do not take such positions. However, things become more complicated when it comes to some of the thorny ethical questions that arise from our growing scientific knowledge and technical ability.

Comparatively straightforward but no less contentious for that is the position taken by the Roman Catholic Church with regard to contraception. It alone of the Christian churches considers 'unnatural' contraception to be wrong on grounds of both 'natural law' and biblical teaching. The Church's position was set out most recently in the 1968 encyclical of Pope Paul VI, entitled *Humanae Vitae* ('Of human life'). It states, in its rather formal language, that contraception is 'any action which, either in anticipation of the conjugal act (sexual intercourse), or in its accomplishment, or in the development of its natural consequences, proposes, whether as an end or as a means, to render procreation impossible'.[6] This includes sterilisation, condoms and other barrier methods, spermicides, coitus interruptus (withdrawal method), the Pill, and all other such methods.

Although Pope Paul, among others, argued that the widespread use of contraception would ruin society and some see the promiscuity of western society as evidence of this, there are many others who would argue that not to allow contraception creates issues of over-large families that increase poverty, can endanger health, and contribute to huge social

---

6. *Humanae Vitae, 14.*

problems related to population numbers. The 'infallible' teaching on contraception must be the most ignored and disobeyed teaching of the Roman Catholic Church. A Univision survey in 2014 carried out across 12 different countries and involving 12,000 responses indicated that 78% of Catholics practised contraception. In some European countries the figure was as high as 90%. Figures on the question of abortion (also forbidden) are considerably lower but still significant. All this reflects changes not only in social attitudes towards sex, women, family size and ways of reducing fertility, but also in attitudes towards authority. The wholesale disregard for a piece of church teaching, especially one that is universally relevant and touches the everyday lives of men and women, undermines the nature of church authority. This in turn can result in a decline in church attendance because people reject a church that is so adamant in its teaching on contraception. Having questioned the Church's authority in one area of their lives, they may well also question its authority to require them to attend church.

Some scientific and technological advances raise ethical dilemmas not envisaged in biblical times or indeed until the modern era. Many of these advances are in the area of the biological sciences where highly complex questions are raised, such as the nature of life, the probity of manipulating the genetic make-up not only of human beings but of other species and plants, the use of chemicals and surgical procedures to alter personality, and the attempts to delay the ageing process indefinitely. At one level many of the products of such research can be seen to have beneficial results for people's health and well-being. But because a thing can be done doesn't mean it should be done. It is possible to so alter the genetic make-up of a foetus that it does not carry life-endangering conditions. But the same procedure could be used to create 'designer babies' in accordance with a predetermined view on, say, what makes a master race. We can clone sheep, so could not we clone humans? It is now possible to place an implant in the brain of a monkey so that it controls, by thought only, an artificial limb in a different room. What questions will this raise when it is possible to do the same in human beings? Leading experts in the world of computers are already warning about the dangers that advances in the creation of artificial intelligence could produce. Once the genie is out of the bottle, there is no way to return it, and what will then be required are ethical decisions about how such advances should be pursued or controlled. But whose ethical principles will be considered?

A sceptical society, where consumerism encourages a mind-set that is dominated by individualism, 'cravings addiction' and rights rather than responsibilities, may look to the scientists, and the entrepreneurs marketing science's products, to help answer the questions. It may be less inclined to look to the churches for guidance – not least if the authority of the churches has already been eroded by their apparent failure to face the realities of modern life.

It is possible to envisage a situation in which the scepticism produced by the consumerist and scientific approaches not only results in a reduction in church attendance but also undermines the churches' contribution to ethical debate that is so vital to society's well-being. And to put it at its simplest: if people do not join religious institutions – that is, not only attend churches but become 'members' – those institutions as currently understood could fold. The Christian story will not have been lost but it will be more difficult to keep it alive and pass it on to succeeding generations. To the extent that this is even a possibility, the decline in church attendance has to be a concern. It will not be reversed unless the churches appreciate at a deep level how the capitalist economic system and the scientific and technological advances influence the way most people think and behave.

In the first section of this book we looked at what we might call the 'popular' reasons people give for not going to church. In this second section we have delved a bit deeper and looked very briefly at two major aspects of modern life – its economic system and the scientific approach to knowledge. While each of these has undoubtedly brought benefits to modern society, they have also raised serious questions for religious faith and have helped to shape mind-sets that result in scepticism about organised religion and the basis of doctrinal beliefs.

In the last part of the book, we will look at some pointers to what might be done and what most clearly to be affirmed in the Christian tradition. Moving from what has appeared to be quite negative, we now consider where there are grounds for being positive. For a faith that has a great deal to say about hope, despair cannot be an option.

PART THREE

SEVEN

Making Connections

It is one of the anomalies of modern society in Britain that, while allegiance to formal religion and church attendance is generally in decline, interest in religion is on the up. More children than ever are sitting exams in religious studies at both GCSE and A-level. In the *Church Times* of 4 September 2015 Peter Graystone wrote this: 'it is interesting to see the 2015 Edinburgh Festival Fringe take Christianity seriously. This year, Christian themes are presented frequently and without cynicism; it is atheism that is exposed as lazy and thoughtless. And audiences have been greedy for it.' Political parties speak openly of the importance of religion both in terms of values and its contribution to ethical debate and in terms of its role in eroding or producing social cohesion.

The Christian churches would no doubt like to think that it is they who have helped to turn the tide. And to some degree they may have, by facing some of the criticisms we saw earlier. But it is largely the increasing religious diversity, created mainly through immigration, that has raised the religious profile. Religion is once again part of the public debate. The extremism of Christian white supremacists or of Islamic terror groups adds fuel to the argument, even if it is an unfair generalisation, that religion is highly dangerous and is a major cause of human suffering. But it has also forced Christians and Muslims, for example, to re-examine what it is that moderates stand for and how they can enthuse people – something the extremists seem quite good at. The challenge for the broadly liberal Christian is to find a way of being confidently and clearly outspoken and not 'wishy washy'.

Seeking to counter one extremism with an alternative extremism will not help. It has been tried and the results are disastrous. The dominant stance has to be one not of confrontation but of conversation, in which each 'side', within or across different religions, speaks with confidence and courtesy and from a desire to discover together a greater truth. We saw something of that humility of 'not knowing' in the scientific approach and how it drives scientists to further discovery. Could it be that this is what is needed among people of faith? While not denying the authority of holy writings and of tradition, it will not be enough to fall back on a literalist acceptance of them. It is a matter of exploring and working with a way of interpreting the heritage of the past and its founding documents that acknowledges religious and secular developments and the play between what is given and what is yet to be discovered.

This debate and discussion will largely take place within and between the religious institutions and, although what they say and do will no doubt percolate into wider society with beneficial results, it may or may not affect church attendance to any large extent. Religious interest is no longer necessarily perceived as involving going to church in a regular and committed way. For that to be reversed would require quite a shift in social behaviour and attitudes. Duty and obligation are no longer the dominant drivers. These days it is much more a matter of individual choice. In the past that choice focused on the question of whether or not to opt out. Today it is much more a question of whether to opt in and that always takes more effort.

When my father was a youngster in the second decade of the twentieth century it was expected that a regular worshipper would attend church twice every Sunday. By the middle of that century regular worship meant going once a Sunday, most Sundays. For many churchgoers today 'regular' means once a month, and this is reflected, for example, in the church attendance requirement for some church schools. 'Occasional' may be as little as once a year at Christmas.

As we saw in chapter one, the statistics of churchgoing indicate that more people attend church services at Christmas than at Easter. The nature of the Christmas story may have something to do with this. Babies and shepherds and wise men catch the imagination much more easily than something as mysterious as the resurrection. While Christmas may, for a Christian, be about the Word made flesh, the coming of the Son of God as a child of Mary, such doctrinal elements are, for most people, of far less interest than the story about a baby. Christmas is a time for children! Nativity services, carol services, Christingle services attract people, and not least families, who seldom step inside a church for the rest of the year.

Is this just sentimentalism, nostalgia, the desire to offset all the commercialism? Maybe in part, but even then it would be worth considering just what is going on. It may well be that in these Christmas services the churches are going out of their way to offer an 'accessible' act of worship. There is a known story, the opportunity for imaginative presentation, familiar music that people can join in with. Usually what is said will be succinct and thoughtful without being dull or too 'deep', and there will be a general atmosphere of good will and welcome. It may be perceived that what is happening on these occasions 'connects' with what is going on outside the church. It fits in with the general feel of celebration that even a secular Christmas has. The services may resonate with something described as 'spiritual' but they don't make too great a demand on those who attend them.

It might be unfairly cynical to say that what is happening here is less about true worship and more about entertainment. But the media have built their readerships and their viewing figures largely on what entertains, and their impact is not negligible in terms of social attitudes and expectations. People do want to be entertained or at least have even serious matters presented in an 'entertaining' way. Entertainment engages. By comparison, Easter is much more a 'church' event – a celebration that makes most sense for those 'on the inside'. The worship will tend to have a greater formality that even Easter bunnies and chocolate eggs will not entirely dispel.

To introduce the notion of worship as having an element of 'entertainment' will no doubt be offensive to some people. But that doesn't mean that there is no validity in it. Perhaps it would be more palatable to say that where churchgoing numbers have increased what is offered at worship is something less formal, less 'head'-focused and more 'heart/spirit'-moving. It is not for nothing that traditional protestantism, and especially its liberal form, has been seen as cerebral and intellectually demanding. It is these churches that are in decline while the charismatic evangelical churches grow. It may give theologians cause for concern but while a word like 'spiritual' gets bandied about more and more, there is less and less precision about what it means and it certainly does not need to be attached to anything approaching doctrinal formulations. Does this indicate a general 'dumbing down' of the whole religious business? Maybe, but it might also show the resilience of that sense that personal experience cannot be exhausted by a secular, functionalist and reductionist view of what it is to be human. We remain 'spiritual' beings. How that is expressed may be far from the language of orthodox and traditional religion. It may even be a long way from what used to be called 'folk religion' which can be seen as a kind of residual 'cultural' memory of Christianity. But churches could do a lot worse than try to understand and tap into what is going on here.

We have seen that there is widespread criticism of the churches, some of it deserved, some it ill-informed. One church that is seldom criticised is the Salvation Army. It may look old-fashioned with its uniforms and military terminology, and people may know little about what it believes, but what they do see is an organisation that cares. In England it is second only to the government in its social care provision. In the 2015 migrant crisis its vans were visible at railway stations and camps, serving out food and drink. Of course they are not the only 'caring' church. Service to the community was built into the parish system. The plight of the destitute, prisoners, child workers, alcoholics, prostitutes and the homeless has motivated both local and national churches to commendable efforts of care and provision. In many cases it has been the churches who pioneered whole areas of social work – much, but not all, of which was taken over by the state and its origins forgotten. The care of those in need runs like a thread through the Christian story. It speaks even when religious words cannot be 'heard'. The simple act of service offered says more about a loving God and a loving community than countless creeds and sermons. And most people, churchgoers and non-churchgoers alike, know that.

A pastor said recently on the radio: 'We need people to know we care before we care about what they know.' This says to me that there is an order of priorities rather than an 'either/or'. People who are not connected to the Church, or are highly suspicious of it, will be more likely to make a connection or overcome their suspicions through loving action than through theological discussion. But while caring is a good in itself, there comes the point where the Christian story and beliefs that inspire and underpin such caring need to be articulated. True loving service is unconditional and not dependent upon what the person in need knows or believes. It is offered as part of the Christian way of obeying the command to love one's neighbour. But Christians also have a responsibility to share their understanding of what motivates that self-giving love in following the example of Jesus. There may need to be great sensitivity and indeed imagination in doing this, but at some point the 'sacrament' of care needs the ministry of 'word'. And this has much to say about how the churches need to help their members not only to know their faith but to share it. It is not insignificant that even in the Salvation Army, known widely for its outstanding community care and stirring band music, numbers are declining. One of the factors has been that, while the general public knows of its 'good works', they are often unaware that the Salvation Army is actually a church, a worshipping community.

If care is important in connecting churches with the wider society, so is welcome. And this needs to be thought about much more radically than simply ensuring that there is someone at the back of the church to say 'hello' to those entering, important as that is.

Radical welcome is both indiscriminate and particular. It is indiscriminate in that *all* are welcome with an equal welcome, but particular in that the welcome sees each as an *individual.* A young mother with three toddlers, a middle-aged couple, a lone teenager, a person in a wheelchair – each has their own needs, gifts and concerns, and for a welcome to feel real some appreciation of these will be needed both initially and on further occasions. Welcome is a process, not just a one-off action. But it goes deeper than this. There are those who come to the church with quite specific requests relating to key moments of their lives – baptism, funeral, wedding. How these are handled is vital – not least because churches may simply not be able to meet every request. But radical welcome seeks to be positive even then. And radical welcome does not wait for people to approach the church; rather, it finds ways to go out to invite and make welcome. It takes the initiative. It does this because its understanding of welcome is grounded in the belief that God goes out in welcome and takes the initiative, inviting all and treating each as an individual.

We have inevitably been moving more and more towards the point where important things have to be said, even briefly, about what the Church believes as well as does, and how those beliefs can themselves form the foundations for what the Church brings and offers to society. It is to this we now turn.

EIGHT

The Gospel Challenge

At the very start of this book we considered the efforts made by the Hallé Orchestra to attract people to its concerts. One of the things we noted was that it remained true to its primary purpose – to perform great music. It did not pretend that its business was really to offer a pop concert. There is nothing intrinsically wrong with performing pop music but that is not the orchestra's purpose. To have done so would have meant losing its integrity and vision. That may mean that only hundreds went to the concert rather than thousands, but simply filling a concert arena is not the primary purpose.

There is nothing wrong with churches being concerned about falling numbers and wanting to attract more people to worship. But the primary purpose is not simply a matter of filling church buildings, regardless of what goes on in them. There may be plenty of room to make worship more accessible, more relevant, more imaginative, more participatory, but if it reaches the point where it is no longer worship it has lost sight of the primary purpose. It is vital that churches are welcoming and find ways of serving the community, but its welcoming and its care still need to be shaped by what it believes Christian welcome and Christian caring to be about. If what the Church does is indistinguishable from what any caring, welcoming, social organisation does, it has lost its distinctiveness. 'The salt has lost its savour.'

It matters what the Church believes, even if it is difficult for some people to accept, and it is important that it speaks with confidence about its beliefs, even if some take offence at it. Having said that, it is not an excuse for authoritarian dogmatism that refuses to listen to the questions the world is asking of it or the criticisms made of it. Retreat into old dugouts will merely perpetuate the atmosphere of antagonism, not open up the necessary dialogue.

What I want to suggest is that, in three vital aspects of the Christian story and understanding, we have a basis that underpins the Church's vision that it offers the world and with which it seeks to attract, invite and welcome into that conversation and participation. Some time ago, I wrote a book that tried to answer the question: 'What is distinctive about church schools?'[7] I concluded that the distinctiveness wasn't so much to do with Christian values as with the beliefs that underpinned those values. The values themselves are largely held in common across all schools, while the beliefs are what is distinctive. So here too I think it is ultimately the beliefs that matter as well as how those beliefs are expressed and lived out. To 'dumb down' those beliefs so that they become no more than a set of clichés for 'nice' behaviour will not do, even if they appear more popular.

This is not primarily a book of Christian dogmatics, so what is offered here is both brief and a taster, a stimulus for further discussion and exploration for those so inclined, focusing on that area of concern discussed in the rest of the book.

In theological terms what I propose to look at are: Incarnation, Crucifixion, Resurrection. In terms of the story of Jesus, this means what we believe the story is telling us in the events of Christmas, Good Friday and Easter.

---

7. John Cox, *More than Caring and Sharing*, Kevin Mayhew, 2011.

Incarnation

The first thing to note is that the coming of Jesus was for the sake of the world, not for the sake of the Church. 'For God so loved the *world* that he gave his only Son.' More than that, he was sent to *save* the world not to *condemn* it (John 3:16-17). At the very least, this means that God's attitude and purpose towards the world is that of saving love. On the basis of the Greek word for salvation, we are talking about the world's wholeness, its health, its ultimate well-being. In St Paul's way of looking at things, the world is seen as set at odds with God.[8] So we can say that even the fact that the world does not view things God's way, that it is even to some extent anti-God, God nevertheless views it with loving concern and wants the very best for it. God sees good in the world even if the world doesn't have much time for God. If that is how God acts, that is how the Church should act. Its attitude to the world should be one of deep loving concern for its well-being, its wholeness.

By implication this also means that the world is not yet whole. In traditional terms, the world is 'fallen'. It makes mistakes, some of them very serious. It is out of loving concern for what has 'faults' that God judges that which is not yet whole. It is not that, in spite of judging, God also loves. Nor does it mean that, in spite of loving, God also judges. It means that God's attitude is one of loving judgement and judging love. Judgement in this sense means the stand over and against that which is not whole but which is the object of love so that it can be transformed. And love is in the sense of a deep and compassionate concern for the world's wholeness which stands with the world in seeking transformation of that which does not make for wholeness. Again, if that is God's attitude, that is what the Church's attitude should be. There is no room here either for a church that withdraws from the world and writes it off, or for a church that uncritically accepts the values and ways of the world.

---

8. See, for example, 1 Corinthians 1 and Colossians 2.

Secondly, incarnation means that it is God who takes the initiative. The movement is from God towards the world and that movement is one undertaken in humility. God comes as a helpless, vulnerable baby. He does not come as an invading general. He does not come as a paternalistic imperialist. He does not come as an exploitative entrepreneur. He does not come in power. The Church would do well to take note of this fact, for over the ages it has used all the ploys of power. A baby does not browbeat those around it. Its demands are those that arise from vulnerability, not from control. A baby has to learn its context and, whatever the Church might say about God's omniscience, the incarnation speaks of a God who learns!

Thirdly, incarnation tells us that God takes the physical world seriously. Matter matters. 'And the Word became flesh and lived among us' (John 1:14). Jesus was not a disembodied spirit or phantom. He was fully physically present. The physical is not just a shell for the soul. The body is not just an encumbrance. It is what Jesus was – a fully physical man. And that means he was as subject as any of us to the opportunities and the restraints of the physical, biological, chemical and neurological nature of what it is to be human as we are. And while that gives humanity a distinctive dignity, because humanity is part of that whole interactive network that is the world and universe in which we live, those aspects of the physical are also of intimate serious concern to God. I take from this the implication that, no matter how much importance we attach to the revelation given to us through the scriptures and through Jesus, we are not to dismiss the discoveries of those who explore, analyse, and measure the physical world. We should also note that Jesus was born into a family, a nation, a culture and a religion. The Church needs to take seriously the context within which it resides and to which it seeks to speak.

Fourthly, the nativity occurred not only at a specific time and place but amidst the political turmoil and violence that too often trouble our world. The Church cannot duck its involvement with world and local events. The baby who was the object of the infanticidal intentions of a tyrant, who was born amidst a subjugated people, who as a child was taken by his parents to a distant land as a refugee, was not a person of high status and privilege. That does not mean the rich are written off but it does mean the poor are God's special concern. He was one of them! The Church is called to have a bias to the poor. But nor can it duck its responsibility to speak out on political and civic matters. MPs may not like the Church having a public voice. There may be a case for the Church of England to be disestablished. But the pressures that seek to make religion a purely private matter are to be resisted. There is a prophetic role the churches still need to take up. It is not their role to simply prop up the status quo of the establishment.

Fifthly, it was not only the political context that was important but that of family and friends as well. Matthew and Luke provide us with information around the birth of Jesus. The Gospels, of course, are not simply telling a story of domestic life. They are making theological points. But for our purposes this, and the fact that Jesus gathered around him disciples and visited the home of friends at Bethany, tell us that Jesus was not a lone guru. Social relationships were important for him. At one level it is common sense to suggest that what was true for Jesus is true for us. But it is increasingly being understood by neuropsychologists, such as the American Dr John Arden,[9] that a lack of social contacts is damaging to our well-being and is actually a contributory factor to, as well as a symptom of, depression. Arden sees what he calls 'social connectivity' as one of five key factors for healthy brains and healthy living. It is among the older generations that this is particularly significant, not least for those who have lost a lifetime partner. When it is stated that attending church is good for people, the importance of social contact is seldom uppermost in people's minds. But its value should not be underestimated.

---

9. John Arden, *The Brain Bible: How to Stay Vital, Productive, and Happy for a Lifetime*, McGraw-Hill, 2014.

Crucifixion

The central symbol of the Christian faith is the cross. We are so used to it that we forget how shocking it is to make an execution post an icon of faith. Of itself it speaks of defeat, of ignominy, of failure. Without resurrection Jesus may well have been admired as a martyred religious wise man but never as the Son of God. It is, as St Paul pointed out, resurrection that makes all the difference,[10] but it is notoriously difficult to encapsulate in a simple symbol. It is only with the eyes of resurrection faith that it is possible to see beyond the humiliation of the cross to its glorious victory and rich significance.

First, we note that Jesus did not go out of his way to be crucified but neither did he seek to escape it when it became the inevitable outcome of his ministry. The way to the cross lay not in what Jesus wanted but in what he saw as the way of obedience to the Father whom he had sought to serve. Such costly obedience was a sign of his integrity, seen so clearly in the agonising struggle in the olive grove of Gethsemane. There are things worth more than self-preservation and personal well-being. There are times when whatever may be seen as rights have to give way to responsibilities. Jesus showed this in all he said and did, but supremely in his willingness to suffer death by crucifixion. The Church may suffer considerably by maintaining a distinctive stand on any number of issues but better that than lose its integrity. Whenever that integrity has been endangered, the Church has been, and rightly so, severely criticised.

There can be a cost to being a Christian. It does make demands – intellectual, emotional and spiritual. It goes counter to the prevailing self-centred focus of so much of our consumerist culture. It might be thought that, in order to attract more people, these demands should be watered down. Make it easier, less demanding. But Jesus never promised it would be easy to be one of his followers – instead he spoke of disciples taking up their cross. The demands are part of what it is to follow the one who gave himself away out of love. Love is demanding. Far from

---

10. 1 Corinthians 15:12-17.

reducing the demand, churches should be outspoken in inviting people into a fellowship of demanding love – and unending grace.

Secondly, we note that Jesus' death on Good Friday has never been understood as the defeat of a hapless victim. Victims are pitied or ignored because of embarrassment. Jesus was not a passive victim. He remained actively doing things, not simply suffering things. And in the things he did he remained true to himself and what he believed. He forgave his executioners, he welcomed a criminal who hung beside him, he thought of the needs of his mother. The Church must not give way to a kind of institutional self-pity, complaining how it has been marginalised, blaming modern attitudes, going on the attack against those of other faiths who have moved into the faith arena. Above all else, it will need to retain the integrity of its best insights, deepest traditions and best actions. It must continue to offer forgiveness, point to the power of lives transformed, speak of God's welcome to all. It must act these out, not just mouth the words.

Thirdly, under the most severe suffering Jesus forgave those who were torturing him. And this characterised what Christians came to believe was the central purpose being worked out through Jesus' death. Whatever theory of the atonement people hold, it comes down to what it says about the nature of love in the face of those who are 'enemies', which in St Paul's view is what we all are in our natural attitude to God.[11] Love risks rejection, it gives everything for the sake of others, it transforms and does not condemn, it invites and does not compel. Self-giving love is the radical nature of power we see in the life of Jesus and supremely in his death. That is its glory and the Church does well to remember this whenever it is tempted to exercise power. History shows it has too often sought other kinds of power. Traditional churches have at times allied themselves too closely to the mores and status of secular authorities and succumbed to the lure of power politics. Newer churches occasionally exercise the power of domination over individuals. Either

---

11. See Romans 5:10.

way the present marginalisation of the Church must not be met by the search for any other power than that of self-giving love.

Fourthly, the Gospels speak of both doubt and trust in the face of death. They tell us that Jesus felt that the Father God, on whom he had always been able to rely, had in fact forsaken him at the point of his greatest need. But they also speak of Jesus' ultimate trust in the God to whom he committed himself. Many people come to church more conscious of their doubts than their faith. They do not always find that the Church is sympathetic or understanding of their doubts. Doubt is too often seen as the enemy of faith while it is certainty that is faith's enemy. In seeking to offer authoritative teaching, the Church will need to do so with an awareness of the place of doubt both in the experience of those seeking faith and in the very nature of faith itself.

Resurrection

Many people bear witness to the fact that God takes them by surprise. There was no greater surprise than the one experienced by the disciples on the first Easter morning. Resurrection is not the inevitable consequence of the crucifixion. It wasn't simply that Jesus rose, he was resurrected. It was the activity of God. And although the Gospels tell us that Jesus had given hints, it was still a surprise, a shock, almost unbelievable. It turned the disciples' grief to joy, defeat into victory, fear into courage. What would have been a dispersed band of despairing, disillusioned disciples became the driving group of the Jesus movement and early Church.

So, firstly, Easter speaks of the power of God to transform situations. There are no guarantees and we cannot predict what the future, God's future, will bring. God will surprise us. All we can do is trust, seek the guidance of the Holy Spirit and act with as much wisdom as we can, while being prepared to change direction if that is what is needed. Trust does not mean doing nothing, but it does mean taking action that is grounded in what we believe about God, about his Church and the world, and acting with integrity.

Secondly, the resurrection was an overwhelming sign of the validity of what Jesus had taught and done. The way of God is the way of self-giving love, not power. What Jesus had taught and done was indeed a faithful expression of the ways of God – a revelation. It had, as it were, the full backing of God and the resurrection was the seal on this. Jesus is uniquely the key to the Church's message and action. The Church from early times has said this – as witness the words of Jesus in John's Gospel, 'no one comes to the Father except through me' (John 14:6). This can, and has been, used to make exclusive claims for the Christian faith and has sometimes fuelled antagonism towards other faiths. Theologians have sought ways to hold to the Jesus claim while discovering the positive points of other faiths and this work will need to continue with added vigour in our faith-diverse world.

Thirdly, the resurrection speaks of both continuity and change. Mary Magdalene failed to recognise Jesus at first. His presence, of course, was unexpected but it was not until he spoke that Mary recognised him. Before that she thought it was the gardener.[12] The couple on the road to Emmaus were joined by a third person, but it was not until he broke bread with them that they realised it was the Lord.[13] Thomas wanted tangible proof before he would accept that this was Jesus.[14] It took time for the fishermen to recognise the figure on the shore.[15] Jesus came to the disciples in strange ways. Doors were shut and yet he appeared in their midst. Having spent time with them he just seemed to disappear. Yet here was the Jesus they knew, bearing the scars of his crucifixion, eating with them, talking with them. The resurrection was something completely new, yet it was not entirely divorced from the past. In the future the Church too will need to work out what it should do in new ways in order to be more accessible, more welcoming, more relevant. It will also need to hold on to what is precious in the past, what is recognisable about

12. John 20:11-16.
13. Luke 24:13-31.
14. John 20:24-28.
15. John 21:4-7.

its core beliefs as it invites people to share its faith and feeds their spirits, as it continues to serve and care for the world.

Fourthly, in traditional language the resurrection made it possible to claim that death had been defeated. Resurrection affirmed the hope that there is more to life than what ends in death. It speaks of a continued, though changed, personal identity – the individual is not simply absorbed into the great sea of existence. It speaks of a change to another way of being alive that does not end but which is mystery – it is not part of a cycle of birth, death and rebirth. It speaks of a life that is fuller than we have known or could imagine – it is not simply a stripping away of all we have glimpsed as being precious and meaningful. It speaks of meaning to life that is not restricted to the particular circumstances of our individual lives here on earth. These are claims made as an act of faith. The Church has good reason to believe they are not fantasies nor simply comforting dreams. They are not provable in the way a scientific proof is but they do speak to the need for meaning which so much of our 'buy quick, throw away' society lacks. In a confident and convincing way, the Church must communicate that, in the gospel, people can find meaning for their lives.

At times it may feel as though the Church is dying. But, as we have seen, the resurrection tells us death does not have the last word – not for individuals nor for the Church, the Body of Christ. What life in the future God has in store for his Church may sometimes be difficult to see, but the promise is for life, not death.